W9-AGD-829

 A co-production by
Bergstrom + Boyle Books
and the Campaign for Real Ale

Beer
naturally

Written by **Michael Hardman**
Photographs by **Theo Bergström**

Beer naturally

Produced and published by
Bergström + Boyle Books Limited
22 Maddox Street, London W1R 9PG
in co-production with
The Campaign for Real Ale
34 Alma Road, St Albans, Herts AL1 3BW

Designed by Tamasin Cole
Cover designed by Richard Rothwell

Text © Michael Hardman 1976
Photographs © Theo Bergström 1976

Made and printed in Great Britain by
William Clowes & Sons Ltd.
Beccles, Suffolk.

Production services by
Book Production Consultants
125 Hills Road, Cambridge.

All rights reserved, including the right of reproduction in
whole or in part in any form.

ISBN Paper 0 903767 09 0
ISBN Boards 0 903767 13 9

Cover photograph: the yard at Jennings Bros Ltd,
Castle Brewery, Cockermouth, Cumbria.

Beer at its best is a reflection of a golden field of barley, a reminder of the rich aroma of a hop garden. Scientists can argue endlessly about the merits of the man-made concoctions which go into much of today's beer but the proof of the pint is in the drinking . . . the best of British beer is produced from the gifts that nature gave us and by methods which have been proudly handed down over the centuries. The story of beer is a story of nature and of craftsmanship; a story of farmers and brewers who join forces to create beer naturally.

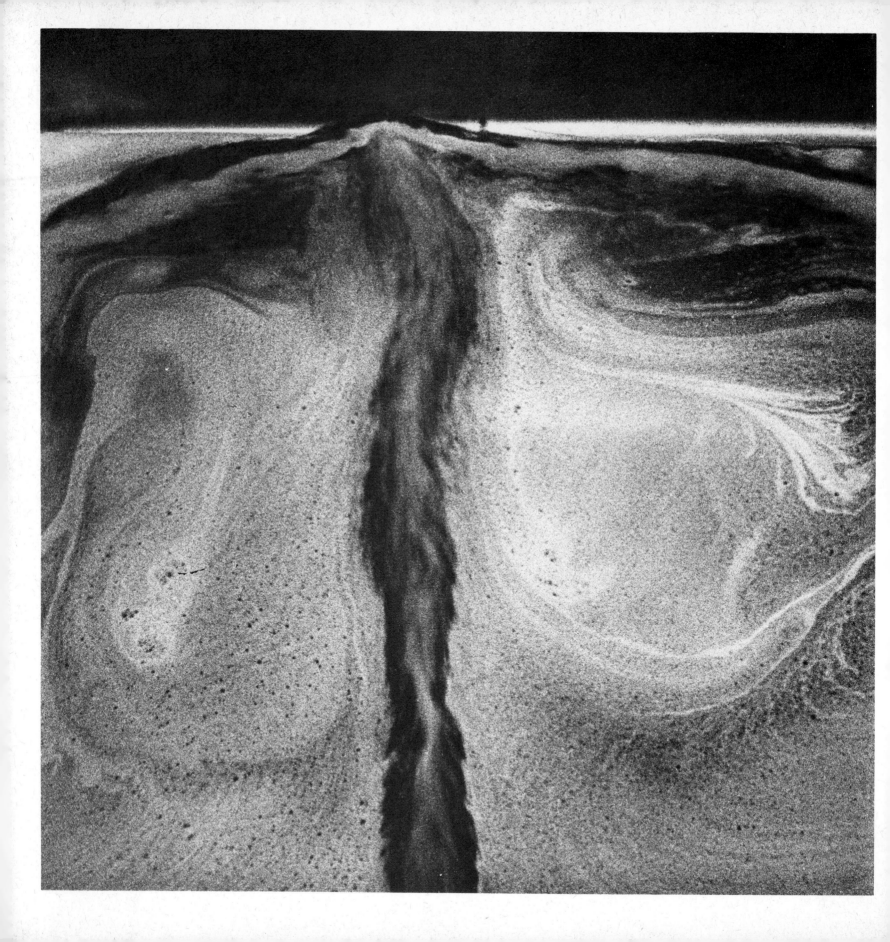

There are a hundred and fifty breweries in Britain, most of them producing at least some beer naturally. The buildings and the equipment inside them come in all shapes, sizes and ages and the methods used vary considerably from one brewery to another. No two beers are brewed from the same recipe and no two brewers follow exactly the same routine in blending the raw materials together, but the basic pattern of brewing is the same throughout the country. Fundamentally, it is a matter of extracting the natural goodness from barley, flavouring the resulting liquid with the bitterness of hops and adding yeast so that the end product ferments into an alcoholic drink.

The story of beer begins in the barley field and the hop garden. It ends, happily, in the pub when the factory worker and the stock broker put their day's work behind them and call to the barman for a pint of beer, naturally.

● *Each photograph marked with a dot also appears in the picture section.*

● Inside the maltings at Paines, St Neots.

● View of Belhaven Brewery, Dunbar, showing the malting towers (no longer in use).

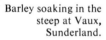

● Traditional wooden malt shovel used in the maltings, standing by an empty steep at Jennings, Cockermouth.

Barley soaking in the steep at Vaux, Sunderland.

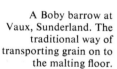

A Boby barrow at Vaux, Sunderland. The traditional way of transporting grain on to the malting floor.

Raw materials

Four raw materials are essential to traditional British beer: barley, which is converted into malt, gives the beer its body and source of alcohol; hops impart bitterness and aroma to the brew and help to keep it free from infection; water accounts for more than ninety per cent of the total content of all beers; and yeast acts to provide alcohol. A number of other substances—both natural and unnatural—are used to varying degrees in many breweries, either to replace the traditional ingredients or to help them.

Barley

Barley, one of the earliest cereals known to man, has been used in brewing since the days of the Hanging Gardens of Babylon and the Pharoahs of Egypt. There is evidence that even in those times, the barley was prepared in much the same way for brewing as it is today, though the methods used were obviously primitive.

Barley is used instead of other cereals because it is easy to grow and is the most suitable cereal for brewing. But it needs to be converted into malt by being steeped in water, allowing it to germinate, and then carefully dried so that the brewer can make full use of the sugar content.

Almost six million acres of barley—a hardy cereal with a distinctive "beard"—are grown in Britain each year, but only about a quarter of the total amount produced ends up in a brewery or distillery. East Anglia is the major barley-growing region, but substantial amounts also come from Hampshire, Oxfordshire, Berkshire, parts of the Midlands and Scotland. The crop is normally sown early in the year, but many farmers try to get the seeds in the ground in the autumn so that the roots will be deep by the following spring, ensuring a hardier crop able to withstand drought.

The farmer who grows barley for malting is looking for a crop which produces grain that will sprout quickly when it is subsequently steeped in water during the malting process. It is also essential that the grain has a high starch content and a relatively low nitrogen content so that the brewer can extract as much sugar as possible. The farmer keeps a watchful eye on the sky, hoping for dry weather in early spring and praying for rain, in moderation, later on. He also has to choose his variety of barley carefully, for he will lose money if his crop doesn't measure up to the standards demanded by brewers. The farmer is helped here by the Brewers' Society, who recommend varieties with names like Golden Promise, Maris Otter and Wing.

Harvesting normally takes place in the early autumn, though barley can now be reaped as early as July. The barley then goes to the maltings, a complex of buildings owned either by a brewery, and often part of a brewery site, or by specialised maltsters.

The barley grains are immersed in large tanks of water until they have soaked up forty to forty-five per cent water. This makes the barley begin to germinate. The moistened grains are then transferred by conveyor or elevator to a germination area where they continue to grow for five to eight days until roots and shoots appear from the hard husk of the grain.

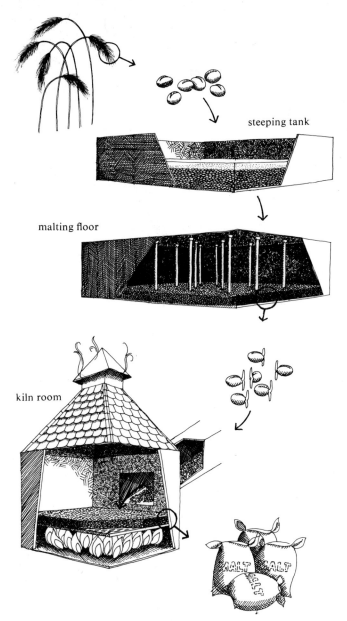

steeping tank

malting floor

kiln room

A malting floor at Paines, St Neots. The steeped barley is floored in the maltings to germinate. After five to eight days it is stripped off and dried in the kiln room.

Turning the germinating barley by machine on the malting floor at Bass, Burton-on-Trent.

Spreading the germinated barley over the kiln floor in the maltings at Vaux, Sunderland.

The drum maltings at Vaux, Sunderland.

In the kiln room at Vaux, Sunderland. Warm air is blown through the wedge wire floor to dry the grain and arrest germination.

Traditionally, the germination area is the floor of a vast hall, where the grains lie to a depth of six inches or so and are constantly turned over with a shovel. But a number of devices designed to save space have been introduced in recent years, including perforated drums which continuously revolve with the grains inside.

The point of germination is to break down the cells of the barley so that their starch content can be converted into the soluble sugars which the brewer needs. The grains must be allowed to germinate long enough to make sure

Barley spread out in the kiln room at Jennings, Cockermouth.

Stringing the hop gardens, using a stringing pole to thread twine through the hooks in the permanent overhead wires and in the ground.

Male and female hop flowers.

that most of the starch content is converted, but not so long that the roots and shoots use up too much of the soluble materials.

When the maltster decides that the grains are in perfect condition, he transfers them to a kiln. The germinated barley is now heated with hot air to about 60° Centigrade (140° Fahrenheit) so that growth is stopped. The moisture content of the grain begins to drop and the temperature is raised to about 70°C (158°F) and later to between 80°C (176°F) and 110°C (230°F), depending on the type of malt the brewer wants. The lower the temperature at the final stage, the paler the malt—and the beer—will be. Malts used to produce the darkest beers, such as stouts, are given an extra kilning at much higher temperatures. In between, there are many varieties of malt, used for making mild ale, bitter, bottled beers and lagers.

The finished product is stored in silos ready for transfer to the brewery malt store.

So the barley, which was of little or no use to the brewer when it left the farm, has been transformed into an easily milled material which can be stored for long periods and—more important—contains the ideal base for beer.

Hops

The Germans and their neighbours were brewing beer flavoured with wild hops more than a thousand years ago and there are records of hops being cultivated in Europe as long ago as 1079. A number of herbs had been added to beer for centuries and passions were high when it was suggested that the hop should take over. In Germany, the centre from which the hop conquered Europe, the new additive was not taken seriously until the thirteenth century and even then, it took time for it to be accepted completely. By the middle of the fourteenth century, Dutch brewers were producing hopped beer, and within a few years they had introduced it to England. British beer was at this stage referred to exclusively as ale and the hopped liquor from the Continent took on the name beer. In 1484, the Brewers' Company demanded that ale should be made only from water, malt and yeast. Nine years later the beer brewers gained recognition as craftsmen in their own right, and for more than a century ale and beer were quite properly regarded as distinct drinks. But hops gradually became accepted, especially when Flemish growers began to invade Kent in the sixteenth century. Hopped beers eventually took over completely from ale and although both words are still used today, they now have precisely the same meaning.

The hop is a climbing perennial plant, grown mainly in Kent, Sussex, Hampshire, and Hereford and Worcester. Altogether about sixteen thousand acres of land are used for growing hops each year. The green cones borne by female plants are used to give beer its bitterness and aroma, as well as to enhance its preservative qualities. British hops have traditionally been fertilised—that is to say the flowers contain seeds—but Continental beers are produced from unfertilised hops. The seeds make little difference to the flavour of the beer, but some popular varieties of hops, with such appealing names as Goldings and Fuggles, produce very small cones when they are sterile. This is one reason why a number of British brewers, and drinkers, are suspicious of Common Market regulations which have created areas of Britain which are free of fertilised hops. Hop growers in these areas must get rid of all male hops, which are never used in brewing but are necessary to fertilise the female hops. Traditional varieties of hops still account for a quarter of the total British crop, however, and it seems that the Common Market regulations will not dictate what kind of hops must be used in brewing in Britain.

Since they are perennial hops are not planted or sown each year, but emerge from the root stumps of the previous year's plant each spring. The hop gardens (or hop yards as they are called in Hereford and Worcester) are dominated by an imposing framework of tall poles, wires and strings. Without this lattice system, the hop bines would trail along the ground and the flowers would be puny. But such is the hop's zest for climbing that it winds around the strings and wires, in some places reaching a height of twenty feet from the ground. The hop farmer has to wage an endless war against insect pests, fungi and viruses before his crop is ready for harvesting in the autumn.

Hop-picking used to be an annual festivity, with hordes of people leaving the big cities for four weeks of fresh air to gather in the hop cones by hand. Mechanisation has almost completely taken over now, and only a few small gardens are still harvested in the old way. Once harvested, the hops must be quickly taken away from the heat and humidity of the autumn air. The cones are separated from the leaves and stems, and taken into a building called an oast house—a familiar sight, with its conical roof and white wind-cowl, in every hop-growing area.

Inside the oast house, the hops are spread in a kiln to a depth of eighteen to twenty-four inches on an open batten floor covered with large horse-hair cloths. The heat in the kiln is steadily increased for three hours and then maintained for a further six hours until the hops are dry. All the time, a fan blows the hot air upwards, through the hops, and out through the cowl. The hops are then spread on the floor of a cooling house for some hours before being packed tightly into large sacks called pockets.

Most of the hops go straight to breweries, but many now go to factories which specialise in producing hop pellets. The factories first reduce the hops to a powder and then compress the powder into small pellets. The qualities of the hop flowers remain unchanged in this process and brewers find the pellets much easier to handle and store than unpowdered hops. The majority of traditional brewers do, however, still use hops straight from the pocket—just as they have done for centuries.

Umbrella stringing pattern.

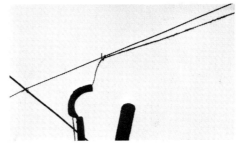

Head of the stringing pole used for stringing the hop gardens.

The four string upright and umbrella stringing patterns.

An oast house, showing the conical roof and white wind cowl.

The well head at Belhaven, Dunbar.

The well under the brewery at Eldridge Pope's Dorchester Brewery. The well is 95 feet deep and the borehole extends for another 500 feet.

The head of the brewing well at King & Barnes, Horsham. Here there is a bore 300 feet deep.

The cold liquor tank at the top of the Hook Norton brewery, near Banbury.

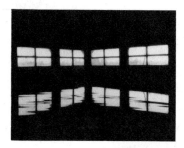

The steam engine, made by Buxton & Thornley, which provides the power at Hook Norton, near Banbury.

Water

Even in the strongest beers brewed in Britain, water outweighs all the other ingredients put together by ten to one; in the weakest beers, the ratio is more than thirty to one. Yet water is often taken for granted by the drinker, who prefers to think of malt and hops as the only constituents of his pint. The choice of water is, however, as important to the brewer as any of the other raw materials, since the impurities which are found in almost every source of supply seriously affect the nature of the beer. Some of these impurities can ruin all the work done in selecting good quality malt and hops; others are totally beneficial.

Brewers realised the importance of suitable water to their products as long ago as the thirteenth century, though they probably had no idea what *made* it suitable. Certain areas of the country became famous for their brewing water as brewers began to base themselves near good wells or running streams. Burton-on-Trent gained a formidable reputation for pale ales because the gypsum content of the local well water helped to produce a first-rate clear beer; London earned fame as a centre for brewing stout because the water from the shallow wells of the area contained a high degree of temporary hardness. But with the growth of population, wells gradually became depleted and rivers polluted, and today the brewer makes more and more use of public supplies.

Burton still has more than fifty brewing wells, however—some of them only 25 or 50 feet deep, taking water from gravel beds; others up to 1,300 feet deep which are sunk into sandstone. The shallower wells provide the classic pale ale brewing water; the deeper boreholes supply water for fuller beers, such as stout.

Brewers throughout the world admire the qualities of Burton water so much that they specially treat their own supplies to imitate its natural gypsum content. This process, known as Burtonisation, is now accepted as an ideal way of combining the purity and consistency of water from public supplies with the chemicals which occur naturally in water from the gravel beds above the Trent valley. Some brewers use different methods of treatment so that their water matches supplies from other brewing centres, such as Tadcaster in North Yorkshire.

The water which goes through the brewing process represents only a small proportion of the total amount needed by breweries. It is not uncommon for ten barrels of water to be used to make one barrel of beer, the other nine barrels being needed for washing the plant, casks and bottles, for steam-raising and for cooling.

Brewing

Many traditional breweries are built like towers, with the brewing process beginning at the top and ending at the bottom, so cutting out the need for expensive pumping systems to move the embryo beer from one piece of equipment to another.

Cold water—or liquor, as it is always described by brewers—is usually stored in a large tank on or near the roof, or outside the building above the level of the machinery inside. When it is needed for brewing, the water is tapped into hot liquor tanks where it is heated up to about 77°C (170°F).

Brewing normally begins in the early hours of the morning and the first task for the brewer in charge is to organise the transfer of malt from the store to hoppers at the top of the brewhouse. Sacks of malt are usually carried up by conveyor belt or mechanised hoist, but some of the smaller breweries have to rely on a hand-operated block and tackle.

The malt is passed through sieves and screens to get rid of bits of root and foreign objects such as nails, wire and dead insects before it is fed into a mill. It is now ground into a grist, ready to be mixed with hot liquor in a mash tun.

When brewing begins, the dry, powdered grist slides down a chute into the mash tun, while a valve is opened to let in the hot liquor. The mash tun is filled almost to the top and the resulting mixture, which looks like thick porridge, is allowed to stand for two or three hours so that the processes that began during malting can continue and the sugars in the malt can eventually dissolve into the liquor. The temperature of the mash begins to drop as time wears on, but the brewer can heat it up again by pumping in more hot liquor through the mash tun's slotted false bottom. If the temperature is allowed to fall or rise too high, or if the time the mash is allowed to stand is not judged correctly, the whole character of the final beer could be altered.

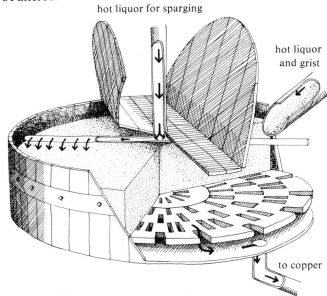

hot liquor for sparging

hot liquor and grist

to copper

Eventually, the liquid is run off through taps under the base of the vessel, leaving behind the hot malt grains

The mill room at Bass, Burton-on-Trent.

The malt mills at Thwaites, Blackburn.

Empty mash tun at Paines, St Neots, showing the sections of the false bottom and the plug for the spent grains. Before the mash tun is filled the sections are laid down on blocks and the tun is filled with hot water to the level of the false bottom to form a base for the mash.

The mash tun at Hook Norton showing the copper funnel which leads from the 'masher' where hot liquor and grist are mixed before reaching the mash tun. When two mash tuns were in use, the funnel could be directed into either by turning the geared wheel.

Mr D. J. Cox, brewer, watching hot liquor and grist, already mixed, enter the mash tun at South Wales United Clubs Brewery, Pontyclun.

Sparging the mash at Paines, St Neots. Hot liquor is sprayed from the revolving arm to extract the last of the sugars from the mash.

The console which controls the mash at Thwaites, Blackburn.

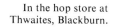

In the hop store at Thwaites, Blackburn.

Equipment used for measuring the hops at Paines, St Neots.

Closed coppers at Eldridge Pope, Dorchester.

Adding hops to the boiling wort in the copper at Youngs, Wandsworth, London.

Sugar in the store at Hook Norton, near Banbury.

which are retained by the slotted base. The brewer then sprays more hot liquor over the bed of the mash from revolving arms in the roof of the mash tun. This technique—sparging—washes away any remaining liquid until more or less clear water comes out of the base. The brewer's judgment and experience are vital at this stage. Too little sparging and there is a danger of leaving behind valuable sugars; too much and there is a risk of extracting other compounds which could spoil the taste of the beer.

Many modern breweries, even some of the medium-sized or small ones, are automated so that considerations such as mashing time and temperature are carefully worked out in the laboratory and adjusted in the brewhouse on an instrument panel, complete with dials and flashing lights. Automation takes much of the risk of failure out of brewing and, so long as the proper ingredients and production methods are used, it shouldn't destroy the character of the beer. It is still possible to go to many a brewery, however, and see human judgment and traditional skills being used at all stages of the process. And nowhere in this kind of brewery is human judgment more important than in mashing.

The sweet liquid that leaves the mash tun is called wort. Five hundred years ago, it would have been run straight into vessels to allow it to ferment into ale, but since the advent—or rather, acceptance—of hops as a bittering agent, wort has had another call to make on its way to becoming our national drink.

It is now boiled with hops in a copper. Most breweries still have coppers made of copper, but stainless steel has been finding favour with some brewers because it is easier to clean.

Hops can be added as soon as the wort is run into the copper, either all at once or, more usually, in portions—some at the beginning of the boil, some mid-way through and some towards the end. They are usually thrown into the copper by hand, straight from a hop pocket, or they can be shovelled in. Sometimes they are weighed into small sacks so that the brewer can be sure of getting the right amount into the copper, and the sacks are merely tipped in through a round hole on the side of the domed vessel. The brewer normally blends a number of varieties of hops together to give the beer the flavour he wants, and occasionally he will use the new season's hops in small proportions, slowly increasing the proportion and at the same time phasing out the old hops, because the bittering substances in hops tend to alter with age.

The more hops that are added, the more bitter the beer will be, though some varieties of hops contain more bittering substances than others. During the one or two hours that the wort is boiling, it is dissolving oils containing various acids from the hop flowers and the brewer has to know how long to let each brew boil to achieve the right degree of bitterness. High temperature often causes some of the more volatile bittering substances to boil off; boiling for too long can reduce the amount of bitterness.

Boiling kills the bacteria in the wort, and it stops the action of the enzymes which broke down the starch of the malt during mashing. The brewer can also take advantage of boiling to put right a deliberate mistake made during mashing. Slightly too much hot liquor is usually sprayed on to the malt when it is sparged so that as much soluble material as possible is extracted, and some of the unwanted liquid can be boiled off from the copper. Another useful function performed by the copper is the precipitation of proteins which could appear in the finished beer as a haze.

Sometimes the brewer will add sugar to the boiling wort to complement the natural sugars extracted from the malt. This practice, which was illegal until 1880, is now widespread, though many brewers proudly adhere to recipes which use only malt and hops.

After boiling the contents of the copper are emptied into a hop back, which has a false base. The hops settle on the slotted base and act as a filter-bed as the wort seeps through.

An open copper at Belhaven, Dunbar.

Another view of the same copper.

A traditional closed copper at Paines, St Neots.

One of the modern coppers at Bass, Burton-on-Trent. Although the front is stainless steel, the inside is copper.

Nearly boiling wort gushing into the hop back at Donnington, near Stow-on-the-Wold.

Mr John Roberts, brewer, washing the simple hop back over the cooling tank at the Three Tuns, Bishop's Castle.

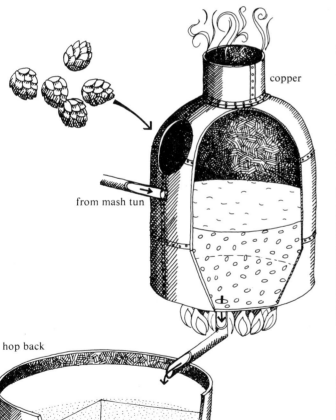

copper

from mash tun

hop back

to cooler

The open cooling tank at Hook Norton, near Banbury. The louvres are opened to increase the circulation of air. The cooling tank is used in conjunction with modern cooling equipment.

A paraflow refrigerator at Paines, St Neots. The hot wort runs from the hop back, over the paraflow and into the fermenting vessel.

● Fermenting vessel and other ancient brewing equipment discovered about ten years ago and now used once a fortnight to produce the Traquair House brew.

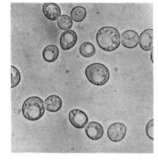

Yeast cells, seen under a microscope.

● Empty fermenting vessel at Paines, St Neots, showing the parachute used for skimming the yeast, in the centre, and the plumbed-in attemperator coil for cooling the fermenting wort.

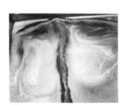

● Wort running into a fermenting vessel at Marstons, Burton-on-Trent.

Yeast is pitched as the wort flows into a fermenting vessel at Marstons, Burton-on-Trent.

The wort is almost boiling as it leaves the hop back and it has to be cooled down considerably before it can be run into fermenting vessels, where it finally becomes beer. In the old days, the wort was pumped to the top of the brewery and allowed to cool in large, shallow tanks, but this method took too much time and the liquid was in danger of picking up bacteria and moulds from the air—not to mention droppings from pigeons in the rafters. Now, compact cooling units, which operate automatically and are highly reliable in controlling temperature, do the job hygienically in no time, though some brewers still have the old open coolers.

Fermentation

The wort now leaves the brewhouse for the fermentation hall—and there is no other stage of the brewing process that can cause so many problems. Mashing is a delicate operation, but a skilled brewer knows when something is wrong and he can normally sort it out quickly. Boiling and cooling are critical to the quality of the finished product, but they rarely present problems if tried and tested procedures are followed. Fermentation can go wrong for no apparent reason, however. It can stop half-way through, fail to start at all or produce obnoxious flavours—and there is little that can be done to put matters right once the process has begun.

Yeast, described by the dictionary as a "yellowish frothy viscous substance consisting of fungous cells developed by germination in contact with saccharine liquids", is made up of millions of individual microscopic organisms which display frantic biochemical activity when they come into contact with sugar-rich liquids such as wort. The temperature of the fermenting wort needs to be rigidly controlled so that the yeast works at the right pace. It must also be kept free from both bacteria and the wild strains of yeast that are present in the atmosphere. Most important of all the fermenting vessel and all pipes leading to it must be scrupulously cleaned between brews.

After the wort is run into the fermenting vessel an Excise officer takes a sample to determine its strength and dips in a long rod to measure the volume of liquid. He does this because brewers pay duty on the strength of the wort before fermentation and he has to calculate how much money to collect on each batch of beer. Every brewery has a little office in the fermentation hall for the Excise man, who is regarded almost as a colleague by the men who make the beer.

Yeast is added—or pitched—into the fermenting vessel, usually from a large drum, and stirred thoroughly so that the whole brew is in contact with yeast. Nine to twelve hours later a fluffy cloudlike foam forms on the surface of the liquid as the yeast begins to multiply rapidly, and within twenty-four hours a thick cream of yeast is thrown up by the millions of bubbles of carbon dioxide gas which are given off as the yeast converts the sugars in the wort into alcohol.

The foaming head of the fermenting vessel at this stage can be almost as deep as the wort below it, and it often seems to be threatening to overflow. When, up to two days after pitching, the yeast head is skimmed off, an ample amount of yeast remains in the wort and fermentation continues.

The yeast is skimmed off either by gently scraping it from the surface with a paddle and channelling it into a chute at the side of the vessel or by allowing it to slip down a large funnel—or parachute as it is usually called—in the middle of the fermenting vessel.

As the same yeast is used time and again in brewing some of the yeast which is removed is pressed and stored at a low temperature and then used to pitch further brews. The excess amount is sold to food companies to make products such as Marmite.

All this activity usually goes on in a conventional open fermenting vessel, but two other kinds of vessel are used in some breweries to produce natural beer—one dating back to the nineteenth century, the other a modern invention.

In the awe-inspiring Burton Union system, which is now to be found only in two or three breweries in Burton-on-Trent, the yeast is pitched in open vessels, but after a day or so the fermenting wort is run into a network of large connected barrels. The yeast head forces its way up pipes, which project from the top of the barrels, and into a trough. This variation on the conventional method was introduced in Burton because it was found to be ideal for the type of yeast used in the town.

The modern invention is the conical fermenter, which is a tall cylinder with a conical base. It saves floor space in the brewery and, because of its shape, the beer tends to complete its journey through the fermenting vessel in as little as two days, compared with the more usual five days and upwards.

In all three methods the rate of fermentation begins to slow down as the sugars are used up, and the yeast suspended in the brew begins to drop slowly to the base of the vessel. When the beer is almost ready to leave a conventional vessel, the brewer makes the remaining yeast drop faster by passing a coolant through a series of coils inside the fermenter. The colder the liquid becomes, the quicker the yeast settles out and eventually only a small amount is left in suspension. The beer, generally described as green beer at this stage, is now near the end of its journey through the miles of pipes, tanks and vessels in the brewery.

Conditioning and racking

It was common practice until the early part of this century for beer to be run from the fermenting vessels straight into casks, where it would be allowed to mature for a few days or weeks before being delivered to the pub. Brewers introduced an extra stage into the process to ensure that the beer was clearer when it entered the casks, so cutting down on the time that the casks had to be allowed to

Mr W.M. Pateman, Head Brewer at Paines, St Neots, beating the yeast with a paddle to reduce its volume.

Mr A. D. C. Webb, the Head Brewer at Adnams, Southwold, inspecting fermentation.

View of the Union Room at Bass, Burton-on-Trent, showing the long lines of connected barrels (unions) into which the fermenting wort is run after 36 hours in conventional fermenting vessels.

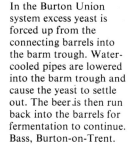

In the Burton Union system excess yeast is forced up from the connecting barrels into the barm trough. Water-cooled pipes are lowered into the barm trough and cause the yeast to settle out. The beer is then run back into the barrels for fermentation to continue. Bass, Burton-on-Trent.

Conical fermenters at Thwaites, Blackburn.

Conditioning and racking

Sluice gate in the copper fermenting vessel at Belhaven, Dunbar. The gate is opened to run off the yeast head.

Skimming the yeast with a paddle at Samuel Smith, Tadcaster, from a slate fermenting vessel.

Yeast press at Eldridge Pope, Dorchester, where the yeast is sucked off the top of the fermenting vessel by a vacuum pump into a yeast collecting cylinder - and then blown by compressed air through the yeast presses.

The tanks at Guinness, Park Royal, where the stout is stored before being bottled.

settle in the pub cellar. This stage, known as conditioning, is the last treatment that natural beer gets in the brewery.

The small amount of yeast left in the beer after it is run from the fermenting vessel is still active in converting remaining sugars into alcohol and carbon dioxide. The beer now goes into conditioning tanks, where the rising bubbles of carbon dioxide produced by continuing fermentation carry with them a number of strongly flavoured substances which cause harsh tastes in unmatured beer. Most of the yeast can be cleared from the beer by the addition of finings, a natural additive made from the swim bladders of certain fish, which drag the yeast to the bottom of the tank. In the old days, finings used to be added when the casks were standing in the pub cellar, but it is unusual now for the publican to handle finings, except in an emergency when the beer has failed to clear.

A sugar solution, referred to as priming sugar, is often added, either to give a sweet taste to the beer or to create the sparkle of natural carbonation during secondary fermentation. Caramel, a form of priming sugar, can be added to give certain beers a dark colour.

Before the beer leaves the conditioning tanks, it is sampled by a panel of brewery employees, who are able to pick out minute changes in flavour. Tasting sessions, in the brewery sample room, also serve as social occasions, but the brewers manage to make their pronunciations on the quality of the beer in a sober fashion because they restrict themselves to sips before socialising.

The casks are filled in the racking plant. Empty casks coming back from the pubs are washed, steamed and inspected to ensure that no rubbish, like old bungs, is still inside. A new bung is banged into the opening on the flat end of the cask and the beer is poured from a hose with a gun-like nozzle, into a second opening—the shive hole—on the curved side of the cask. A handful of hops, or a made-to-measure hop pellet, can be dropped into the beer at this stage to improve its aroma as it continues to ferment in the pub cellar. Most breweries also add finings when the beer is being racked, even if they have been used during conditioning. Once the cask is full, a bung is driven into the shive hole and off it goes to a store or direct to the loading bay.

Five sizes of cask are in common use in brewing today: the pin ($4\frac{1}{2}$ gallons), firkin (9 gallons), kilderkin (18 gallons), barrel (36 gallons) and hogshead (54 gallons). A number of metric casks—of 50 litre or 100 litre capacity for example—are now being introduced, but the old Imperial sizes with their fascinating names seem likely to be with us for years to come, for no better reason, perhaps, than the cost of replacing such expensive items of equipment all at once.

Casks can be made of wood or metal, and some are lined with nylon or plastic. The material used makes little or no difference to the taste of the beer: some brewers prefer wood because it is easier to repair, it insulates the beer from heat and it is more attractive than metal; others plump for metal because it is cheaper, considerably lighter and easier to clean. Breweries with a large number of wooden casks have their own cooper's shop, where new casks are made and old ones repaired. Even though the number of coopers has dropped drastically with the acceptance of metal casks in the past ten or twenty years, the ancient craft is still alive in a handful of breweries.

Bottled beers are almost always subjected to processes such as filtration, pasteurisation and pressurisation, which sterilise the beer and change its flavour significantly, but a small number of brands are still bottled in their natural condition. The best known are the nationally available Guinness Extra Stout, Worthington White Shield and Courage Russian Stout, though a few local breweries also produce natural beer in bottles: the rare and potent Thomas Hardy's Ale brewed by Eldridge Pope of Dorchester and Prize Old Ale brewed by Gales of Horndean, Hampshire, are two examples. The yeast is still alive in all these bottles, though most of them, with the notable exception of White Shield, are so dark that the sediment cannot be detected. White Shield is pale and clear, however, and the brewers recommend that it should be poured out carefully so that the sediment is left at the bottom of the bottle along with a small amount of beer.

The bottling hall of even a small brewery is an amazing place. Seemingly endless snakes of bottles rattle their way on rollers and conveyors around a battery of machines to be washed, filled, labelled, crown corked and put into crates automatically.

At the loading bay, casks and bottles are piled on to lorries, or drays as they are called, for delivery to the pubs—and the beer is almost ready for drinking.

In the pub

The time and skill which the brewer has given to his cherished product on its path through the brewery has to be matched by an understanding, or even love, of the beer and its peculiar patterns of behaviour on the part of the licensee of the pub where it is to quench a thousand thirsts. Nothing must be done to the beer to ruin the flavour that the brewer has worked so hard to get right.

Casks of beer can be set up in two places in the pub: in the cellar or in the bar. In either case, the cask needs to stand for a day or two so that the sediment in the beer—consisting mainly of yeast and hops—settles to the bottom. The cask is laid on its side and held securely in position on a cradle or gantry, or kept steady by means of chocks pushed under its curved belly. A tap is hammered into the bung on the flat end of the cask and a wooden peg called a spile is knocked into the soft core of the shive at the top to allow the carbon dioxide gas produced by the continuing fermentation of the beer to escape. Spiles come in two varieties—soft and hard—and the landlord has to make sure that the right one is in the cask at the right time. The soft spile lets out a lot of gas when the beer is fermenting quickly; the hard spile controls the output of gas more rigidly and stops the

Cask washing at Paines, St Neots.

Cask washing at Marstons, Burton-on-Trent.

Sniffing the cleaned barrels at Samuel Smith, Tadcaster.

Apprentice cooper in the cooper's shop at Samuel Smith, Tadcaster.

Cooper making staves at a mule. Samuel Smith, Tadcaster.

In the pub

The racking line at Bass, Burton-on-Trent.

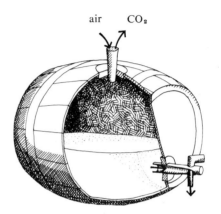

Racking at South Wales United Clubs Brewery, Pontyclun.

Finings being added to racked casks at King & Barnes, Horsham.

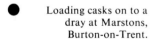

The ale store at Bass, Burton-on-Trent.

Loading casks on to a dray at Marstons, Burton-on-Trent.

beer going flat. Large pubs employ their own cellarman, who is expert at manipulating spiles so that the beer is always in tip-top condition, as well as generally looking after the cellar and making sure that enough beer is available at any one time to satisfy demand. The cask needs to be drained quickly—within a few days—to prevent the beer going off as air is drawn in through the spile to displace the liquid drawn off. But a good landlord will make sure that the casks he orders are not too big to be drunk by his customers within the prescribed time.

Many seasoned drinkers vow that the best way to serve beer is by gravity, straight from the cask. The big advantage of this kind of service is that the beer doesn't need to travel through pipes or pumps, which always need to be spotlessly clean, but the landlord has to be careful that the beer doesn't get too warm, especially when it is stored in the bar in hot weather.

The ideal temperature for storing beer in the pub is around 14°C (57°F) and this is where the cellar comes into its own. Publicans and brewers realised long ago that beer would keep better if it were stored underground, away from the humid atmosphere of the bar, and almost every pub now has its own cellar or another room which is artificially cooled to fulfil the same function. A few licensees make a trip down to the cellar to draw off the beer by gravity, but the vast majority rely on pumps to pull the beer up to bar level and into the glass.

The pumps used to serve beer naturally in England and Wales fall into two categories: manually operated and electrically powered.

The manual variety, described by most drinkers and licensees as handpumps, raise the beer through a beer engine, which is a straightforward suction pump hidden underneath the bar counter. Each time the handle on the bar is pulled, beer issues forth from the cask, through the pipes and into the glass. Any amount of beer can be delivered at varying speeds, but a complete pull of the handle usually serves up half a pint. In the North of England, where beer has always been presented with a long-lasting, tight head of froth, handpump spouts are often fitted with nozzles, or sparklers, which can be screwed up tightly to force the beer through a tiny opening at high pressure. In the South, where beer has always had a flatter appearance, the spouts are left wide open, so that the beer comes out with a loose, foaming head. The difference between the two methods of service is a matter of taste and habit. The end product in either case is very much the same, though the Northern system gives a smoother texture to the pint and the Southern method a more easily distinguishable flavour.

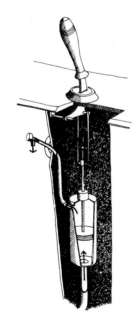

Electric pumps find favour mainly in the North and Midlands, where bigger pubs with high turnovers have identified a need to cut down on the energy-sapping aspects of handpumps. A good barman or barmaid can pull two or more pints at the same time through electric pumps, thus being able to serve the customers more quickly. The pumping mechanism is housed near the barrels in the cellar and each time the tap is operated at bar level, an electric motor is activated, with the beer being pulled up to the bar in much the same way as it would be by a beer engine. The commonest type of tap associated with electric pumps meters the beer into half pints (or occasionally into pints) through a glass cylinder or sphere mounted on the bar. A diaphragm moves back and forth each time a handle is pushed to one side, ensuring that the contents of the cylinder or sphere are pushed into the glass. A considerable amount of electrically pumped beer is, however, dispensed through extremely simple taps, which activate the motor for as long as they are pulled—an arrangement known as a free-flow dispenser. Both the metered and free-flow varieties of electric pumps can be operated by a push-button system, though this is rarely used to serve natural draught beer.

In Scotland the majority of natural beer is served by air pressure. The old system, which lingers on in a few bars, is operated by a water engine, a contraption like a lavatory cistern which converts mains water pressure into air pressure and pushes the beer through tall metal taps or fonts on the bar. Most pubs now use electric air compressors, which do exactly the same job.

In spite of their vastly different appearances and methods of operation, all these systems of service have one thing in common; they keep the beer in its natural condition and preserve the flavours and characteristics that the brewer tried to achieve in the first place. So long as the beer

Serving beer by gravity at the Black Horse, White Roding, Essex.

Typical pub cellar — underneath the Flask in Hampstead.

An electric pump mounted on the floor beneath the casks.

Two types of taps used to dispense electrically pumped beer: metered (left) and free flow.

Bottling Thomas Hardy's Ale – the strongest beer of any kind produced in Britain – at Eldridge Pope, Dorchester.

Measuring the original gravity of the wort in a fermenting vessel at Bass, Burton-on-Trent.

The excise dip – a brass plate which marks the place where the Customs and Excise officer measures the depth of the wort in the fermenting vessel to calculate the volume of the brew.

In the laboratory at Thwaites, Blackburn.

is stored at the right temperature and the cask is properly vented by correct use of hard and soft spiles, and provided that the pipes from cellar to bar are always clean, little can go wrong.

The strength of beer

The strength of beer can be measured in two ways: by its original gravity or by the proportion of alcohol.

Original gravity is a measure of the amount of fermentable material added to water to make beer. The density of water is rated at 1000 degrees, so that a beer brewed at 1036 degrees will have 36 parts of fermentable material to every 1000 parts of water, and so on. Original gravity is calculated before the wort begins to ferment, so it only gives an indication of the body of the beer and not necessarily its strength when it reaches the glass. It is, however, the measurement on which excise duty is based and it is a good guide to value for money as it shows the ratio of water to other materials used in the brewery. The weakest beers in Britain have an original gravity of around 1030 and the strongest are above 1100. The average bitter is brewed at between 1035 and 1040 and it is unusual to come across a beer brewed above 1050, except for winter brews, barley wines and special strong ales.

The measurement of alcohol content is usually based on volume. Average beers have an alcohol content of 3 to 4 per cent; the weakest are around 2 per cent; and the strongest above 10 per cent.

The strength of beer should *never* be used to judge quality. Strong beers are not necessarily the best—or rather the most suitable for an individual's own palate—nor are weak beers necessarily the worst. Some low-gravity beers have an abundance of natural flavour and are just the thing for a long session in a pub. Many high-gravity brews are, on the other hand, disappointing; they give the impression that they have been brewed with little regard for flavour, as though strength were the only criterion. The reverse is, of course, often true, and the only way to judge the quality of beer is to drink it.

Beer unnaturally

British brewers are practically free to tamper with their beer as much as they want, unlike their colleagues in West Germany, who are forbidden by law to use any ingredients other than malt, hops and water, and in the Isle of Man, where the Government has outlawed a host of substitute materials and methods. Fortunately, many brewers in Britain have kept faithful to nature, and beer brewed and served naturally can be found in almost every corner of the country. On the other hand, the past fifteen years or so have seen a proliferation of brewing ingredients and processes which have resulted in more than three quarters of our beer being nothing like the drink which has borne the name for centuries.

The brewers have turned their backs on tradition for two reasons: to save money at a time when British beer carries the highest tax in Europe and the price of hops and malt has been rapidly increasing; and to make their products easy to handle to the extent of being foolproof.

Unmalted barley, wheat flour, flaked maize and even potato starch have been used in mash tuns in addition to malt. These cheaper ingredients, known as adjuncts, tend to produce beers of a different character if used in large quantities, though most brewers use them only as a small proportion of the grist. Some companies produce their beers entirely from a substance called malt extract, which is a thick concentrated preparation of the sugars contained in malt grains. Brewers argue about the effects of using malt extract instead of mashing, but a comparison of the taste of two beers, one produced naturally and one from extract, should be enough to convince any drinker that the scientific debates miss the point.

The swing to short-cut brewing has also seen the development of hop concentrates—thick, treacly extracts of natural hops—which brewers often find more economical to use than whole hops and which also cut out the need for personal judgment and skill when the wort is boiled in the copper. Like malt extracts, hop concentrates generally make for uninspiring beers.

The most frightening variations from traditional brewing involve a number of processes aimed at producing beer faster and cheaper. Two of them involve fermentation. Natural beer is fermented in batches in open vessels, but some of the big brewers have in the past few years opted for a process of continuous fermentation in which the wort passes endlessly through a high concentration of yeast. In one system, the wort enters at the base of a tower and by the time it reaches the top, it is completely fermented beer. The brewer not only gets his beer more quickly from a continuous fermenter; he also saves time and money on cleaning out fermenting vessels after each brew, since continuous fermenters can run for several weeks without stop. But there are major problems in keeping the tower sterile and sophisticated apparatus is needed to control the rate of flow, aeration and temperature. Most important of all, the quality of the beer suffers, since the speed of fermentation makes a marked difference to flavour. The brewers have even been tampering with conventional batch fermentation by adding chemicals called antifoams to the wort to prevent a large, foaming head from forming. The idea is that the brewer can fit much more wort into his fermenting vessels if the head doesn't rise.

Even beer brewed from natural materials and by conventional methods can be subjected to unnatural processes before it leaves the brewery.

The traditional addition of finings to beer to pull the natural sediment to the bottom of the container has been replaced in many breweries by filtration. The beer is first stored in large tanks and chilled so that most of the yeast sinks to the bottom and is then passed through a filter which removes any remaining solid particles. Beer processed in this way is described as chilled and filtered or bright beer. At least one brewery does, however, manage to filter its beer only partially, so that some yeast remains to ensure that a secondary fermentation takes place in the pub.

The advantage of filtered beer is that it doesn't need to settle before being served. It can also be transported from brewery to pub in large road tankers and piped into cellar tanks which hold the equivalent of several barrels. It is close to being the answer to the brewer's and publican's prayers for a stable beer which needs little or no skill to serve.

The ultimate answer to these prayers is provided by the process of pasteurisation, which finally kills off all remaining life in beer after it has been filtered. The beer is heated up to 65°C (150°F) for a few seconds, which is enough to put an end to even the hardiest of life which survives filtration. The beer is now completely sterile, but it has a different taste from natural beers.

Natural, unprocessed beer stored in a cask produces carbon dioxide as it continues to ferment and, so long as not too much or too little of the gas is allowed to escape through the spile, the beer will be in perfect condition—not too fizzy, not too flat—when it is served. But beer which has been filtered and pasteurised is incapable of producing its own carbon dioxide. It would be flat and lifeless if it were served up without an injection of gas, so it has to go through a further process either in the brewery or in the pub cellar. Keg beers, which are always filtered and usually pasteurised, get their name from the sealed containers in which they are stored. Kegs are normally pressurised with carbon dioxide before they leave the brewery and the beer is forced into the glass simply by opening a tap on the bar and letting the gas force it through the pipes. Beer served in this way is fizzy, and the high level of gas disguises the lack of natural flavours which were removed during filtration and pasteurisation. Keg beer is much the same as bottled beer, since nearly all bottled beers are filtered, pasteurised and artificially carbonated in the brewery.

Unpasteurised but filtered beers are either sent to the pub in kegs or in road tankers and then pressurised in the cellar by coupling the container to a cylinder of carbon dioxide to keep air away from the beer and to displace the liquid drawn off. The result is a less fizzy pint than the pasteurised and highly pressurised beer usually stored in kegs, though the quality is considerably lower than well kept natural draught beer.

Even unprocessed beer in a cask can be pressurised when it gets to the pub, either to prevent air getting to the beer through the spile hole (blanket pressure) or to force the beer from cask to bar (top pressure).

Many brewers argue fiercely in favour of processed and pressurised beers because they are more consistent than natural brews and it seems that many drinkers have accepted them with no complaint. But they are not the same as beers brewed, treated and served naturally. They are missing the taste of the barley field and hop garden.

A large brewery such as
Bass of Burton-on-Trent
employs a team of
plumbers to maintain
the miles of pipes and
vessels in the brewery.

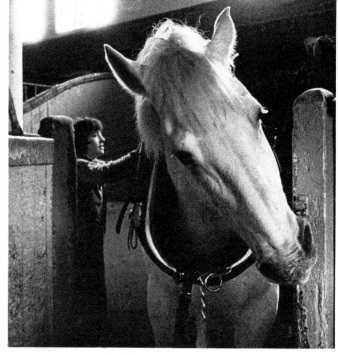

Dray horse in the
stables at Vaux,
Sunderland.

● Mr Peter Maxwell
Stuart (Laird of
Traquair) and his
daughter Catherine who
helps him with the
brewing.

● The brewer's office at
● Hook Norton, near
Banbury.

● Mr Bill Monk, Head
Brewer, Jennings,
Cockermouth.

● The Three Tuns brewery
at Bishop's Castle.

A Drinker's Dictionary

Some common words and phrases used in the brewing industry

A

Adjunct: ingredient other than malted barley used in mashing, such as flaked maize, unmalted barley, wheat, pasta flour and potato starch.

Alcohol content: measure of the amount of alcohol in beer, usually expressed as percentage by volume rather than weight.

Ale: originally used in England to describe unhopped malt beverages, as distinct from beer, which was brewed from malt and hops; ale and beer now have the same meaning.

Alpha acid: one of the bittering substances contained in hops.

Antifoam: a compound usually of silicon, used to prevent fermenting wort from forming a large, foaming head; used to make greater use of the capacity of fermenting vessels.

B

Barrel: cask of 36-gallon capacity.

Batch fermentation: the conventional system of allowing wort to ferment into beer in separate batches, rather than passing it continuously through a concentration of yeast.

Beer: see Ale.

Beer engine: suction pump, consisting of a piston inside a cylinder, operated by a handle on the bar of a pub; used for raising beer from the cellar.

Beta acid: one of the bittering substances contained in hops.

Bitter: well hopped pale or amber beer of average or fairly high gravity.

Blanket pressure: a layer of carbon dioxide applied to the top of a cask of beer from a cylinder connected to the spile hole; used to cushion beer from the air, but not to propel the beer to the bar.

Boiling: bringing wort to the boil in a vessel called a copper while hops are added.

Bottom fermentation: traditional Continental method of fermenting wort, used in lager-brewing; a strain of yeast which sinks to the bottom of the beer is used instead of the kind used to ferment British beer, which rises to the top.

Brewery conditioned: description of beer which has been filtered and maybe pasteurised in the brewery instead of being allowed to ferment, or condition, in the cask or bottle.

Bright beer: see Chilled and filtered.

Brown ale: beer brewed from dark malts, usually bottled and often of low gravity.

Burtonisation: the treatment of water with certain chemicals to make it similar to the hard water which occurs naturally around Burton-on-Trent.

Burton Union: system of fermenting wort now found only in a handful of breweries in Burton-on-Trent; the wort is fermented in a series of large connected barrels instead of in open vessels and excess yeast is forced up into a trough, leaving the beer comparatively clear.

Butt: cask of more than 100-gallon capacity; no longer in general use.

C

Caramel: form of burnt sugar used for adding colour to beer.

Carbon dioxide: gaseous compound of carbon and oxygen produced by fermenting beer; injected artificially into processed beers.

Carbonation: the process of injecting carbon dioxide artificially into beer.

Cask: conventional container which stores draught beer at atmospheric pressure; it has two openings—one to let the beer out; one to allow carbon dioxide to escape as the beer ferments and air to enter as the beer is drawn off.

Cask conditioned: description of beer which is allowed to condition completely in the cask instead of in the brewery conditioning tanks.

Cellar tank: large container fixed in a pub cellar and holding the equivalent of several barrels; the beer is piped into the tank from a road tanker.

Centrifuge: machine which rotates at high speeds; used in a brewery to separate solid particles from beer very rapidly.

Chilled and filtered: description of beer which is free of solid particles; the beer is first chilled so that solids such as yeast sink to the bottom and then passed through a filter to get rid of any remaining particles.

Chit malt: a Continental malt, produced by restricted germination.

Chocolate malt: dark malt which is roasted after being kilned.

Cold liquor tank: container used to hold water before it is heated for the first stage of brewing.

Collar: the frothy head on a glass of beer.

Conditioning: period when beer continues to ferment after being drawn from the fermenting vessel; beer can be conditioned in the brewery, in the cask or in the bottle.

Conical fermenter: new cylindrical design of fermenting vessel, with a conical base, aimed at saving space and time in the brewery as well as improving hygiene.

Continuous fermentation: new process whereby wort is passed endlessly through a concentration of yeast, instead of being allowed to ferment in batches in open vessels.

Cooper: craftsman who makes and repairs wooden casks.

Copper: vessel made of copper or stainless steel, where wort is boiled with hops.

Crown cork: metal disc which is pressed around the top of a bottle instead of a stopper.

Crystal malt: specially kilned, medium dark malt, rich in natural sugars.

D

Double rackings method of running beer from one container into another so that the sediment stays in the first container.

Draught: term generally used for any beer which is delivered through a tap or pump but correctly applied only to beer which is **drawn** from a container by gravity, beer engine or electric pump. (The dictionary says that anything described as draught should be drawn.)

Dray: wagon used to carry casks and bottles from brewery to pub.

Dry-hopping: putting a handful or pellet of hops into a full cask of beer before it leaves the brewery to improve its aroma.

E

Electric pump: motor operated by electricity which draws beer from cask to bar at the flick of a switch.

Enzymes: natural materials produced from barley during germination which convert proteins and carbohydrates in the grain into soluble nitrogen and sugars.

Extracts: preparations of malt or hops used instead of natural materials.

F

Fermentation: the process of converting wort into beer by allowing yeast to change the natural sugars into alcohol and carbon dioxide.

Fermenting vessel: large tank where fermentation takes place.

Filtration: removal of solid particles from beer by passing it through a filter unit.

Fined: term used to describe beer which is made clear by the addition of finings.

Finings: substance which is added to beer to drag solid particles to the bottom of the container; see Isinglass.

Firkin: cask of nine-gallon capacity.

Flash pasteuriser: piece of equipment used to sterilise beer by subjecting it to heat.

Free-flow dispenser: tap which allows beer to flow as long as a handle or button is depressed; used to dispense either electrically pumped or pressurised beer.

G

Gantry: wooden frame which holds casks steady in the cellar.

Gravity: method of delivering beer to a glass direct from a cask; see also Original gravity.

Grist: powdered malt, ready for mashing.

H

Handpump: a beer engine.

Head: the foam on top of a glass of beer.

Hogshead: cask of 54-gallon capacity.

Hop: climbing perennial plant; the cones borne by the female are used for giving beer a bitter flavour.

Hop back: equipment used to strain wort through hops after boiling in a copper.

Hop extract: soluble bittering substances extracted from hops and concentrated into a syrup.

Hop garden: plot of land where hops are grown.

Hop pellets: compressed hop powder.

Hop pocket: large sack used to contain hops.

Hop powder: natural hops finely shredded for easy storage.

Hop yard: term used instead of hop garden in Hereford and Worcester.

Hot liquor tanks: containers where water is heated ready for mashing.

I

Invert sugar: the commonest of the sugars which may be added to wort during boiling to complement natural sugars extracted from malt.

IPA: see Pale ale.

Isinglass: whitish semi-transparent substance obtained from swim bladders of fish, especially sturgeons, and used in beer as finings.

K

Keg: sealed container for processed and pressurised beer.

Kieselguhr: substance commonly used as a filter aid.

Kilderkin: cask of 18-gallon capacity.

L

Lager: light-coloured beer of Continental origin, produced by bottom fermentation at a low temperature and stored for long periods before being served; nearly always processed and pressurised.

Light ale: term used by some brewers for bottled pale ale.

Liquor: brewers' term for water.

M

Malt: barley grains which have been allowed to germinate after being steeped in water and then heated in a kiln to arrest germination at a point where the grain is ideal for brewing.

Malt extract: preparation of sugars extracted from malt and normally concentrated by heat into a syrup; used instead of natural materials.

Maltings: complex of buildings where barley is converted into malt.

Malt mill: machine which grinds malt grains into a powder called grist.

Malt screen: apparatus which removes roots and foreign objects such as nails before the malt is milled.

Maltster: man or company operating maltings.

Mashing: process of extracting natural sugars from malt by mixing it with hot water.

Mild: lightly hopped beer usually of low gravity and either light or dark in colour.

N

Naturally conditioned: term used to describe beer which continues to ferment in the cask or bottle.

O

Oast house: building where hops are dried after picking.

Old ale: beer which has been allowed to mature for several months or even years; usually of high gravity.

Original gravity: measurement taken before fermentation of the amount of fermentable solids added to water to make beer; expressed in degrees, based on a gravity of 1000 for water—hence beer with an original gravity of 1036 has 36 parts of solid material to every 1000 parts of water; Excise duty is payable on gravity, so you can expect to pay more for a higher gravity beer.

P

Pale ale: beer brewed from pale malt, usually of medium gravity and served on draught or in bottles; India Pale Ale or IPA, generally a good quality bitter, got its name because it was able to withstand sea voyages to India.

Paraflow refrigerator: kind of wort cooler.

Pasteurisation: method of sterilising beer by subjecting it to heat.

Pin: cask of 4½-gallon capacity.

Pitching: adding yeast to wort.

Pocket: see Hop pocket.

Pressurisation: artificial addition of gas (usually carbon dioxide) to cask or keg of beer.

Priming sugar: sugar, usually in a solution, added to beer during conditioning, either to give it a sweet flavour or to create a sparkle during secondary fermentation.

R

Racking: filling casks with beer.

Re-racked beer: see Double racking.

S

Sample room: part of brewery where beer is tasted by experts (and visitors).

Secondary fermentation: natural process whereby beer continues to ferment in cask or bottle.

Shive: wooden or plastic bung with penetrable central core which allows carbon dioxide to escape from cask beer through a wooden peg called a spile.

Skimming: action of removing yeast from top of fermenting beer.

Sparging: spraying hot water over malt in a mash tun to extract additional sugars after initial liquid has been drained off.

Sparkler: adjustable screw which can reduce the width of the opening on the spout of a handpump to force the beer out at high pressures; used for giving the beer a tightly knit head of froth.

Spile: wooden peg knocked into the central core of a shive to control the amount of carbon dioxide given off by beer; soft spiles are porous and allow gas to escape quickly—hard spiles retain more gas.

Stillage: a cask is said to be on stillage when it is securely positioned on a gantry or held steady by chocks to allow sediment to settle to the bottom of the beer.

Stout: dark beer of medium to high gravity, brewed from roasted malt.

T

Tank: see Cellar tank.

Top fermentation: traditional British method of fermenting wort by using strains of yeast which rise to the top of the beer during the initial period of fermentation.

Top pressure: artificial application of carbon dioxide to the top of beer in a cask to force it to the bar.

Tun: obsolete cask of more than 200-gallon capacity; also see Mash tun.

U

Underback: area below a mash tun which collects wort after mashing.

V

Venting: control of carbon dioxide escaping from cask of fermenting beer by using hard and soft spiles.

W

Water engine: device used in Scotland to raise beer from the cellar by air pressure.

Wort: unfermented beer.

Y

Yeast: tiny fungous plant, visible individually only under a microscope; used to ferment wort into beer.

CAMRA, the Campaign for Real Ale

The Campaign for Real Ale was formed in 1971 to fight for an improvement in the quality and availability of beer brewed and served naturally. It now has a membership of 30,000 enthusiastic beer drinkers throughout Britain and almost 150 local branches, run entirely by voluntary effort.

CAMRA's only financial support is from membership subscriptions, the sale of publications on beer and brewing, and the sale of products such as ties and badges. Yet it has managed to save thousands of pubs from the threat of conversion to processed and pressurised beer, and has persuaded hundreds of others to switch back to natural beer after years in the wilderness. Many brewers have given moral support to the Campaign by declaring that they will continue to brew and promote real ale and others have begun to reverse their previous policies of producing nothing but processed beers.

But there is still an enormous amount of work to be done. Nine pints out of every ten drunk in Britain are brewed by seven giant companies, all of whom have put more and more faith in keg and pressurised beers over the past few years. Only about a third of the country's 70,000 pubs sell natural beer, and even some of that is disappointingly low in quality. CAMRA's battle can only be won when every pub in Britain is serving at least one traditional beer, and this can only be achieved with the support of beer drinkers everywhere.

Details of CAMRA membership can be obtained by writing to the Membership Secretary, CAMRA, 34 Alma Road, St Albans, Hertfordshire, AL1 3BW.

Breweries featured in this book

1. Belhaven Brewery Co Ltd. Dunbar, Lothian.
2. Traquair House, Traquair, Peebleshire.
3. Vaux Breweries Ltd, Sunderland.
4. Jennings Bros Ltd, Castle Brewery, Cockermouth, Cumbria.
5. Daniel Thwaites & Co Ltd, Star Brewery, Blackburn, Lancashire.
6. Samuel Smith Old Brewery (Tadcaster) Ltd, The Old Brewery, Tadcaster, North Yorkshire.
7. Bass Production Ltd, Burton-on-Trent, Staffordshire.
8. Marston, Thompson & Evershed Ltd, Shobnall Road, Burton-on-Trent, Staffordshire.
9. Three Tuns, Bishop's Castle, Shropshire.
10. Paine & Co Ltd, The Counting House, Market Square, St Neots, Cambridgeshire.
11. Adnams & Co Ltd, Sole Bay Brewery, Southwold, Suffolk.
12. Hook Norton Brewery Co Ltd, Hook Norton, Banbury, Oxfordshire.
13. Donnington Brewery, Stow-on-the-Wold, Gloucestershire.
14. South Wales & Monmouthshire United Clubs Brewery Co Ltd, Crown Brewery, Pontyclun, Mid Glamorgan.
15. Arthur Guinness Son & Co Ltd, Park Royal Brewery, London.
16. Young & Co's Brewery Ltd, Ram Brewery, Wandsworth, London.
17. King & Barnes Ltd, 18 Bishopric, Horsham, West Sussex.
18. Eldridge, Pope & Co Ltd, The Dorchester Brewery, Dorchester, Dorset.